Our Bible

Martha Durepo • Illustrated by Pat Karch

Broadman Press
Nashville, Tennessee

For
Laurie Anne Durepo
and
her Daddy and Mommy,
Randy and Robin
whose lives she brightens

© Copyright 1987 • Broadman Press
All rights reserved.
4241-75

ISBN: 0-8054-4175-1
Library of Congress Catalog Card Number: 86-17571
Dewey Decimal Classification: C220
Subject Heading: BIBLE

Printed in the United States of America

Library of Congress Cataloging-in-Publication Data

Durepo, Martha, 1940-
   Our Bible.

   (Bible-and-me)
   Summary: A simple introduction to the Bible as a book about God and Jesus, one with stories about them and others.
   1. Bible—Juvenile literature. [1. Bible]
I.Karch, Pat, ill. II. Title. III. Series.
BS539.D87   1987   220.6'1   86-17571
ISBN 0-8054-4175-1

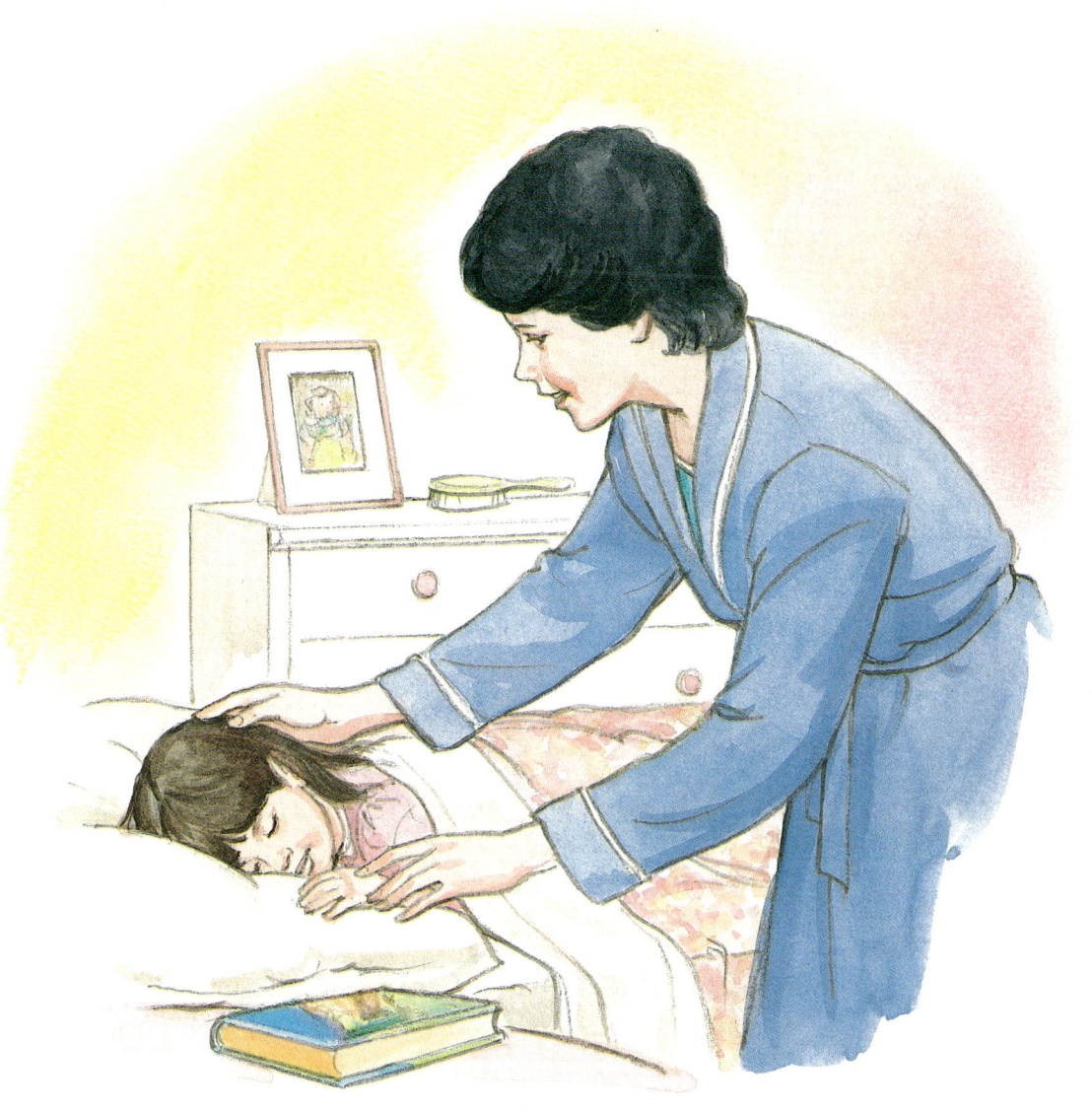

"Wake up, Laurie," said Mommy. "It's time to get ready to go to church."

"I like to go to church," Laurie sang as she held her kitten.

In our Bible we read, "God gives food to us." "Thank you, God, for Laurie's cereal," said Daddy.

"Mommy has a Bible. Daddy has a Bible," said Laurie. "We are going to church."

"Good morning, Laurie. I'm glad you came to church today. Our Bible tells us Jesus went to church."

"I love Laurie, I'm glad she came to church," sang Miss Gail.

Laurie, you and Brad are painting with red. Our Bible tells us God made many things that are red. Thank you, God, for red strawberries and red apples.

Our Bible says, "Help one another." Laurie is helping with the baby. Andy is helping cook the food.

Our Bible says, "We are helpers." Laurie and Marilyn are being helpers when they put the blocks where they belong.

"We open our Bible and what do we see?" sang Miss Patsy.

"A picture of David and his woolly sheep."

Laurie, you may help me strum the autoharp. "I am happy, I am happy, Laurie has come to my church," sang Mr. Bill.

Our Bible says, "Love one another."
"I like to go to church," said Laurie.

Look, Laurie. I see birds in the tree. Our Bible tells us God made birds and trees. "Thank you, God, for birds and trees."

Laurie, you worked the puzzle all by yourself.

Our Bible says, "Work with your hands."
Thank you, God, for hands.

Brad, I will whisper a Bible verse to you, then you may tell the others.

"Be kind to each other," said Brad.

"Miss Gail gave me a Bible marker for my Bible," said Laurie.

Here in our Bible is a story about a boy named Samuel. Samuel helped his teacher.

"Daddy, please read me the story about Timothy in our Bible," said Laurie.

Goodnight, Laurie. Daddy and Mommy love you. Our Bible says, "God loves you, too."